Preface

I concede that this is rather long to detail a singular, simple solution. In piecing together my thoughts, I have erred on the side of thoroughness. I felt that such a simple solution required explanation as to WHY it will work, and, why other solutions haven't or won't. I also realize that anyone reading this might be familiar with some of the information I'm presenting. I've included those parts anyway, because just as many might not be familiar with them.

I also want to point out that the first step to solving a problem is that all involved must actually WANT to solve the problem. As I began talking to people about this idea, I started wondering if people (on either side) truly want that. Both sides say they want greater safety, but do they really? As a society, we have much to gain with greater safety. Both sides also have much to lose if this issue was suddenly resolved.

Everyone expresses a desire for that greater safety. Yet, with so much to gain for all of us, both sides seem more invested in maintaining the fight. If a real solution was presented, would anyone actually be interested? It appears, as divided sides, there is infinitely more to gain by perpetuating the fight, regardless of what we'd gain as individual citizens. By keeping solutions at arm's length, blaming the other side, both sides have a multi-million dollar mission. There are millions of dollars given in hope. A solution ends the mission. What would people do with all the energy and money invested if this problem was resolved?

I have discussed this idea with hundreds of people since 2014. Everyone I have talked to, on both sides, with few exceptions, loves this idea and believes it will work just as I claim. I present my idea with great hope that the person reading this will support the idea and help create a snowball of action. Sadly though, I have low expectations. I present the idea because it has become something I could not NOT do.

And, I am aware that before any action could take place, this idea will need some work. Research will be needed to confirm the points I make, thoroughly vet the idea, and prepare the idea for implementation, as well as minor customization for some regions. I would LOVE to be part of the team that does that work. My passion for a solution compelled me to write this. It is my hope to be included in the next steps towards application of the idea I've written about.

David Hendrix
Chicago, Illinois
May 2022

My Perspective

I love studying history, and the history of our amazing country is a must read. Studying history has made me a strong supporter of our constitution. The rights of the citizens should never be abridged. However, just as we have to keep in mind the genius of our founding fathers, we have to balance that with remembering what the world was like when they wrote it, as well as the reasons for what they wrote.

Our constitution is one of the most intelligently crafted documents ever. The thinking that went it to it is pure genius. I believe it reflects the great intelligence and foresight of the authors. However, their greatest brilliance was in creating a LIVING document that was ready to evolve and grow and mature as our country evolved and grew and matured.

Almost everyone in my family, as far back as I can remember, has owned at least one gun. Most had several. Most of my friends have had guns. That said, I have never owned a gun personally and have never fired one. I've never felt a need for one. I have been fortunate that I've never been in a situation that I believe a gun was the solution. I'm perfectly comfortable around guns (as long as they aren't aimed at me). I've just never needed one myself.

Being exactly in between the two sides has given me a unique perspective on the issue. I am truly able to see the merits of both sides, as well as the shortcomings. It is from this perspective that I present my idea.

A Little History

We didn't win our independence by whooping the Redcoats. In some battles, sure. But mostly, we won by making the cost of the fight greater than the British were willing to pay. That was accomplished because ordinary Americans, and anyone who could be recruited, had a gun or two, and literally, every single person in the colonies was able to join the fighting force. Our "well regulated militia" consisted of many private citizens, many of whom had little, if any connection to the formal army. Victory cemented this into a cornerstone of our country. Soon, we got our Constitution and this cornerstone became our Second Amendment.

The revolution really was a David vs. Goliath situation. The British were the best trained and best equipped in the world. We barely had an army at all, and what we had really wasn't especially well-trained. I'm pretty sure it wasn't Washington's plan to win that way. But, it worked. It was a type of war that the British weren't prepared for. Behind every tree, there was a farmer with a musket. Every house had a handful of people ready to defend against the Redcoats. This is a strategy that people have used ever since when a more formidable army invades their homeland. It still works in virtually every country.

Many gun advocates hold on to this strategy as a primary reason they are so passionate about the 2nd Amendment. IF they are ever needed to defend the homeland, against enemies foreign or domestic, they'll be ready.

Anyone who has studied law will recognize this strategy. A plaintiff doesn't need to win. They just need to make the cost of the case greater than a settlement with the defendant. This strategy, even if it isn't recognized as coming from the American revolution, is commonly used.

"A well regulated Militia, being necessary to the security of a free State, the right of the people to keep and bear Arms, shall not be infringed."

Now, even without the NRA and other advocacy groups, this cornerstone has become so much a part of our identity, as a nation, that to change it would be a dramatic makeover of who WE are, as a nation. As our young nation expanded West, a gun was as common and necessary as a hat and boots.

The Cornell Law School has published some good history of Supreme Court rulings regarding the 2nd Amendment and guns.
https://www.law.cornell.edu/wex/second_amendment

Media outlets such as USA Today, Everytown for Gun Safety, The Washington Post, CNN and other television news sources, as well as Shooting Tracker and Mass Shooting Tracker, cannot even agree on the statistics and the definition of a "mass casualty shooting incident". Crime statistical sources also cannot seem to be consistent. Everyone can all agree that incidents are becoming more frequent and more deadly. But, that's all we seem to be able to agree on.

My personal opinion is that one of the greatest challenges we have in resolving this issue is that we cannot agree on a modern adaptation of the founder's words. The 2nd

Amendment says, "the people", but doesn't specifically say, "individual citizens". It says, "Militia" but doesn't define what a "Militia" consist of. It clearly says, "well regulated", but those on the right get most heated and those on the left are the least satisfied when we discuss what exactly "well regulated" consist of. I get nervous when I think about the U.S. government regulating anything because the track record isn't always up to the challenge.

In 1776, they had no way to imagine the current situation. And because the world has evolved the way it has, we CANNOT hang on to a single, 250-year-old sentence as gospel, as wise as the founders may have been. WE have to evolve to meet the challenge we are faced with today. I'm definitely not saying to throw out the 2nd Amendment or any part of the U.S. Constitution. I'm just saying we have to rethink how we adapt the words to a modern world. That has to begin by everyone getting on the same page, with the same goal.

As It Stands...

"The largest mass-casualty event in American history." I heard this on the news over and over and over and over in reference to the shooting in Orlando. And later, the shooting event in Las Vegas. Every time I heard that sentence, I had two thoughts. The first is that somewhere in America, there is an individual sitting in their home, watching the wall-to-wall news coverage, just like me, and thinking, "Challenge accepted." It might be a lost high school student who has been bullied. It might be a wannabe terrorist. It might be a racist or bigot of some kind. It might be someone with mental health issues. For fame. To make a statement. To pledge allegiance to a cause. It could be anyone. The only thing we can be sure of is that their goal will be to increase the body count. That event is coming. The person who will commit that horrific act has canonized the shooters in Orlando, Sandy Hook, San Bernardino, El Paso and Colorado going all the way back to Columbine. They are his heroes. And despite the exemplary efforts of law enforcement - even if they do everything right - we are unlikely to see the event coming and be able to prevent it.

The second thought was that how many people have to die in a single event before we - as a society - do something different? As it stands, there's no solution in sight, with an ever-widening chasm between the two sides, we are setting the stage for increasingly more horrific events. After each one, everyone cries for an answer. No answer comes.

As it stands, we are getting further and further polarized on this issue. With every shooting, the right digs in further. With every shooting, the left screams louder. Legislation has completely failed to stop the shootings. Debate has failed to stop the shootings. Protests have failed to stop the shootings. And worst of all, continuing to fight about it has failed to stop the shootings. Following the recent shooting in Uvalde, legislators have taken some great steps. However, the steps they have proposed are not much different than previous legislation and fail to address the issue with a true solution. Improvement, maybe. Solution, nope.

It is time to consider a new idea. Taking all the guns away is not the answer. The "An armed society is a polite society" mentality is not an answer. Both of these are grounded in hubris. Our answer lies in intelligently rethinking the issue. And with some humility, we must be determined to find the answer - even if that answer requires compromise on both sides.

Currently, we do not have such humility and determination.

In The Red Corner...

All of the first Amendments to the Constitution were, first, to protect the citizens from a failed government, and second, to give the citizens the means to start over should the government fail its citizens. In regard to the 2nd Amendment, they weren't thinking about a shooter in a movie theater or market, and certainly not a school. They weren't thinking about home invasions by thieves. They weren't thinking about rival drug dealers and gangs. Those things were truly unimaginable in 1776.

What they COULD imagine was Ol' King George crossing the pond again and putting the kibosh on our independence. It may seem like a far less considerable threat now. But defense of the homeland, is most effectively carried out by a well-armed homeland. This fact was true then, and now, here, and in every other country in the world. We may think of it as a less important role of the 2nd Amendment these days, but looking around the world at other countries in conflict teaches us that citizens being able to play a role in the defense of their homeland is as relevant today as ever.

Our founding fathers could also imagine our democratic experiment failing horrifically. The Bill Of Rights gave the people the necessary tools to deal with either of those situations. Then, and now, those tools keep our government honest and in service to The People, rather than us in service to the government. So, we need ALL of the Bill Of Rights, working individually and as a collective, to keep the United States the greatest country ever.

There is also an extension of the thinking among 2nd Amendment advocates that any weapon the government has, the citizen should have the right to that weapon as well. If the citizens are truly going to keep the government honest against tyranny, or in the event of a government that fails its people, the citizens need to be able to arm themselves equal to the government. For example, if the government has a tank, the citizen should be allowed to have a tank. Or an F-16. A nuclear powered submarine, even nuclear weapons. Technically speaking, this is a fair interpretation, even if it is an interpretation that takes the law to an exaggerated extreme.

A less exaggerated interpretation can be applied to assault weapons.

Advocates that wave the 2nd Amendment also state, "An armed society is a polite society." In theory, that argument has merit. If I know my neighbor has a gun, I'm going to choose my words carefully when I approach him about his dog crapping on my lawn. I'm going to think twice before I flip the bird to the driver who just cut me off in traffic when I consider that he might have a gun. The core of this thinking is that if everyone has a gun, potential shooters will think twice before they act. And if they do act, the surrounding citizens will be able to neutralize that shooter quickly.

The Problems With The Red Corner

Knowledge that YOU have a gun, makes me want to keep mine handy and at the ready. Just in case. Both of us can be reasonable, intelligent people. But if we have a conflict, pointing guns at each other reduces us to cavemen hitting each other with sticks and rocks. No one wins when we escalate the likelihood of shooting each other. Imagine the person with road rage. Imagine the person whose laptop died 3 days after the warranty expired and Best Buy won't honor the guarantee. Imagine the guy who got fired from his job, unfairly in his opinion, whether it's true or not. These are "normal" people. Not mental patients. Not terrorists. They're just average Americans who have been told by our societal mores that if you have a problem, show them your gun because you don't have any other options.

Sadly, the theory of most people respecting each other leaves a person with an unresolved feeling when they don't see something as fair. When a person feels unresolved, they are MORE likely to reach for their own equalizer instead of seeking a reasonable solution with their neighbor. Will they really think twice in the heat of the moment? Overwhelmed with a feeling of hopelessness at finding a fair resolution to a grievous wrong (real or imagined), I think history has shown that more and more people are reaching for a gun without a second thought.

How polite will we be when the neighbor has a rocket launcher? I mean, technically, he can have one. Right? And if his dog craps on my lawn one more time, I'll get me one too. Detente among the citizenry doesn't make us happier and safer. Mutually assured destruction only guarantees the standoff - and eventual launch - not a resolution to any conflict.

Imagine the staff at the movie theater in Colorado, all armed and ready to take out a shooter in a dark theater full of other people, also armed with guns. Over 200 people all shooting at one guy in the dark. Am I the only one terrified of that image? A possible 20 to 30 killed by the shooter, and another 50 killed by friendly fire trying to neutralize a single target.

Give guns to flight attendants. One or two terrorists on the plane with eight guns pointed at him. Surely the terrorist would get shot. Surely. But I also think surely someone is going to depressurize the plane, too.

Imagine the grocery store. One guy comes in to rob the place and 100 shoppers all whip out their guns as the perp ducks down the cereal aisle. Honestly, when I think about all these scenarios, I become terrified of getting shot. Not by criminals or terrorists, but by "normal" people all trying to do the right thing.

In the Blue Corner...

The left doesn't really care about the guns. Not exactly. They care about the deaths. They care about the lack of action and the lack of results. They care about the hardheadedness of gun advocates and their stranglehold on politicians. They care about sending their kids to school and having that little voice in their heads that reminds them of all the school shootings we have had. They care about going to a mall, or to church, and being afraid.

They care about the stalemate that we are stuck on and how the legislation so far has not reduced the deaths and has not made anyone feel safer.

What drives their argument is that the United States has more shootings than every other country - combined. We have more in a single year than all of the next 50 countries have in a 5-year span.

If we can reduce the number of deaths and restrict the ability of individuals who are more likely to do harm with a gun, the left will likely be reasonably satisfied. The objective that they really want is to have confidence in our safety. When they leave their house - their children, their loved ones and the people in their community - they just want to be confident that they will safely arrive back home.

The most logical solution to address the problem is to reduce the number of guns. They look towards other countries who have strict gun laws and logically, draw the conclusion that the same action will work here. Fewer guns = fewer gun deaths. This is math that SHOULD add up. It makes sense and it's the conclusion that the left is generally driving towards.

The Problems With The Blue Corner

Legislation that restricts gun purchasing has not accomplished the goal of reducing gun violence. Further legislation will not accomplish it either. Ask the cities that continue to have gun violence issues in spite of strong legislation. How do we define insanity? To continue with the same ol' action expecting different results.

The answer is not more gun "control". It hasn't been very effective thus far. The laws that have passed have failed to stop gun violence. And, when those laws fail to accomplish the goal, it gives the gun advocates backing when they resist more and more gun control laws. The overwhelming majority of gun owners are responsible people who we never need to worry about. Why should laws be aimed at them, when the dangerous individuals comprise such a small percentage of gun purchasers?

We had a ban on assault rifles for a while. It curbed assault rifle use. It did NOT curb overall gun violence. Every agency and organization that records such things, confirms that assault rifles are a small part of the overall gun violence we have, even though the news networks will sensationalize it otherwise. So, the ban didn't really make as big of a dent in the overall problem as supporters claim. Recent shootings were with assault rifles, and the ones that make the news always are. But overall, assault rifles are just one of many guns being used.

"Make it a crime to have a gun and the only people with guns will be criminals." The statement has the deeper meaning that gun owners who are now law abiding will be, by definition, criminals. Another common interpretation is that only criminals will remain holding guns, not average citizens who are compliant. It seems to be the weapon of choice for school shootings, but for the overall problem, AR-15 rifles are a small part. A lot of people simply WILL NOT give up their gun(s) and will then be classified as criminals. There's some accuracy to both of these interpretations and a lot of misunderstanding.

What if we just take ALL the guns away? When we start trying to take guns from Americans, the Americans with guns will start shooting. They have made that clear. We could have Wacos all over the country. We will also create an even larger black market for guns than we have now.

In Australia and the UK, they have strict gun control and comparatively little gun violence. However, we are not them. What works there, will not work here because the 2nd Amendment has ingrained gun ownership for the entire lifespan of our country. We have a history of gun ownership that further perpetuates and grandfathers in a culture of gun ownership in a cycle of philosophy, not just practice. I personally fear that trying to take people's guns will be catastrophic. It could possibly be civil war level.

Or, imagine if we tried to repeal the 2nd Amendment.

Last, when you say "control", I admit I bristle a little. It doesn't matter what it is you're wanting to control and how much I might support such control. "Control" is not something I want as a free citizen of the United States. Or, just as a human in general. The rebellion thing runs deep in American people. No wonder we can't get very far with this issue. Everyone gets defensive when we introduce the word.

A Parallel Issue

A car is a 4,000-6,000 lb weapon that causes more deaths each year than guns. We turn 16 year olds loose with an SUV the size of a small house and NOBODY has a problem with that. And, we do that knowing that the 16 year old doesn't have the maturity or mental capacity to make grown up decisions regarding the impact of his own behavior on the population around him. The 16 year old, experimenting with his new freedom, thinks he's 10 feet tall and bulletproof and that accidents only happen to people who aren't as smart as he is. Thus, he thinks it's okay to text, drink, smoke pot (or worse), eat, flirt with a girl, laugh with his friends, all while he's responsible for that SUV. Where are the huge lobbying groups fighting over his rights to do that or to take the keys away?

There aren't any. We, as a society, recognize that some common sense must be used when we hand those keys over. The 16 year old must pass a test and have a little training. Some states have additional restrictions until the kid is older. And, we have rules for driving. Speed limits, red lights, don't text, don't drive under the influence, no racing in the subdivision, wear a seatbelt, etc. All of which are enforced reasonably well, effectively and fairly by the police. Driving, for the most part, is well regulated and we are all okay with how that is done. We AMEND the rules regularly as driving and vehicles evolve.

No one has a problem when a young man loses his license for his failure to follow the rules. We have no problem with that young man paying a high rate for insurance because he is more likely to be risky. We have penalties that are more severe when a person is irresponsible and injures (or kills) other people. AND WE ALL AGREE TO THIS. Yes, there are some who want the rules or penalties tweaked. But, for the most part, we all agree to the same basic driving rules. Across the country. Across party lines. Race, gender, age, sexual orientation, economic or social background, we all mostly agree to the same basic rules and no one has a problem with it.

Why can't the same model be applied to guns? I'm sure I'm not the first to see the parallels of these two issues.

Could the acceptability of regulation and a set of laws lie simply in the perception of driving as a "privilege", not a "right" or an entitlement as we have with guns? Could the issue boil down to semantics?

Gun Responsibility

The answer is to require:

1)   Strict, FEDERAL registration

2)   A safety test on the weapon you want to buy prior to the purchase

3)   **YOU MUST HAVE INSURANCE ON ALL GUNS**.

Nothing else. No other laws. No other restrictions. One law, as simply worded as possible, in effect repealing and superseding all other gun legislation. No riders. No padding. No add-ons. One FEDERAL law. If you want a gun, any gun, as many guns as you want, go buy that gun or those guns. But, you must register it, you must assure others that you know how to safely operate it, and you must carry insurance on it. Period.

Registration would consist of a file created with the gun's serial number and a rifling pattern. The gun owner, annually, would renew the registration. They would verify their address and contact information and sign a statement that they will be responsible for the gun they are registering. This statement should, as a reminder, list the consequences of their gun being used improperly. The states will handle the task of gathering and maintaining this information in a UNIVERSAL manner. Yes, the federal government and ALL law enforcement agencies worldwide will have access to this information.

Guns that have no serial number, cannot be registered and thus, are illegal. Those guns will be destroyed immediately upon discovery and the person in possession of that gun will suffer serious FEDERAL consequences.

No more guns "falling off the back of the truck". This registration process begins with the manufacturer. Every gun produced is registered with the manufacturer as the owner. When that gun is transferred to a distributor, wholesaler, reseller, the registration follows and is transferred to that person. If YOU, the wholesaler, are listed as the last person to register a gun that is later used in a drive-by, YOU will hold some responsibility. And THAT is the operative word: responsibility. Having a strict registration process begins to engrain that word. And having it begin at the top of the system, it builds a mindset that follows down the line.

Operating tests can be designed by the manufacturer, combined with input from law enforcement and recognized gun experts. The tests should be fair, but MUST demonstrate the proper and safe operation of the gun and general gun safety. Classes might be offered by dealers and sellers, and even manufacturers. The result might be an increase in gun sales, which is fine, as long as the buyer has shown they can handle the weapon safely and intelligently. A test must be completed for each gun purchased. If two of the same model gun are purchased at the same time, one test is sufficient. If they are purchased separately, a separate test must be completed. Two different guns? Two different tests. These tests should be repeated periodically, possibly every 5 or 10 years, if the person still owns the same gun.

The insurance will cover any liability of the gun owner. Insurance companies will draft a variety of policies to cover the gun owner with the gun they purchase. They can ask questions, make rules, whatever they need to do to feel confident in insuring the gun owner. They will assess the RISK of that individual with that gun and charge a price for coverage. Coverage will consist of, for example, if the gun is used to shoot someone without cause, or if the gun is used in a crime. It would also cover theft. It would also cover property damage or injury in an accidental firing of the weapon. The insurance should also cover providing a criminal or civil defense, provided that the insured has complied with all requirements of the insurance contract. Policies could be customized for varying needs and individuals as long as they cover basic liabilities required by law.

The cost of the insurance would be determined by several items. It would weigh factors with the gun such as the caliber of the bullets fired by the gun, muzzle velocity of the bullets as well as the amount of damage that can be done to a human being and/or property. In addition, the cost of the insurance would consider factors of the insured individual who is buying the gun. Factors that generally indicate responsibility would decrease the price of that insurance policy. Factors that generally indicate a higher risk would increase the cost of the insurance policy.

This will not eliminate all gun violence, no more than requiring car registration and insurance has eliminated all drunk driving and driver irresponsibility. What it has accomplished is to GREATLY REDUCE those issues. It has created a punishable offense that no one questions. It has created a standard that we can all accept. It has given us a framework to work on solutions as needed, adapt as auto transportation changes, and create peripheral laws that reduce the irresponsible use of an automobile. We do not have such a framework now with guns because we are so polarized.

We start off with everybody having the right to have a gun, just as the 2nd Amendment is interpreted. Some things will restrict the type of gun you can have. You have to pass the aforementioned test, for example. The more damage a gun can do, the more advanced the test you must pass. And, the consequences and penalties are greater depending on the gun. You buy a single shot hunting rifle that really won't even scare the deer, it comes with a very low standard to meet. You want to buy a Browning .50, a much higher standard is required.

Personally, I understand the interpretation of the 2nd amendment that implies that I have the right to have any weapon the government has, even if this interpretation is ridiculous. We're not talking about farmers providing a well-defended homeland against the Redcoats with muskets anymore. If we are truly going to keep the government honest against tyranny, I might need a couple of tanks for that. Or an F-16, or even something with a little more kick. I don't have a tank. I'm not even thinking about buying one because I don't have the skills to operate it. However, if I could pass a test that shows I can be responsible for one and can operate one in the manner that it should be used for, I should be able to have one by this extreme interpretation of the 2nd Amendment. Just in case.

Imagine what the insurance would be though. The insurance on a tank, as a potential weapon, would be astronomical. It might actually cost more than the tank. And, if I am determined to be a little risky because I am considering the purchase of a tank, it's quite possible that no insurance company will be foolish enough to underwrite that policy. Without the insurance, my tank stays with the original owner. Risky behavior, as determined by the insurance company, could prevent the purchase of an AR-15, or a 9mm by the same individual. And yet, would provide no barrier whatsoever to someone with a history of responsible behavior.

I have the same problem with driving an 18 wheeler. There's a test for that and I'm pretty sure I wouldn't pass without a whole lot of training. I rented a truck to move and the guy showed me how to make turns and change lanes and park without running people over. Lots of training. I didn't get that when I bought my car. Shouldn't the same standard apply for a weapon that can remove a limb with a single shot? Or a gun that can wipe out a cafeteria full of school children? A test doesn't seem like so much to ask. And consequences, if you fail to live up to what was required when you passed the test, should be expected.

This is America, land of the free. You want a gun? Go get a gun. Just give the rest of the population some confidence that you won't shoot us with it. To me, that seems like a reasonable request.

An Intelligent Solution

If we are going to be intelligent with our guns, we have to be intelligent with how we view the issue. This is what we need to do with gun ownership. Reduce the violence by reducing the likelihood of the wrong person having a gun. The insurance requirement will do that. But also, by changing the mindset of gun ownership. Instead of it being a polarizing issue with no compromise, we can change the way gun ownership is understood by both sides.

When it is viewed as a RESPONSIBILITY (still protected by the 2nd Amendment), we are more likely to be more responsible and do the things that responsible people do. When we view it as a RIGHT (which it is, guaranteed to all Americans), "right" somehow becomes "entitlement" and it demonstrates why we are lobbying and advocating and arguing for everyone to have a gun when some people are clearly not able to be responsible with it.

That may sound like semantics. But choices of words and emphasis will change the perception. Now, we emphasize "rights", and thus, the rights are what we argue about. When we emphasize the responsibility of gun ownership, the conversation changes to those responsibilities. This change in emphasis will also serve to soften the divide and polarization because we have the focus on the true issue of what is needed. I'm sure both sides can agree that the divide isn't solving the problem. A collective focus on responsibility could possibly unite both sides.

Insurance companies don't talk about rights or about taking guns away. They talk about liability, risk and responsibility. By involving insurance companies, we will immediately change the language of the debate to something that both sides agree on from something that divides everyone.

The overwhelming majority of gun owners are responsible citizens. They take gun ownership seriously. They are VERY aware that a gun is a weapon and use of such a weapon is not something to take lightly. If we look at the shootings that have occurred, they are seldom (if ever) committed by typical gun owners. They are committed by people who have little regard for the U.S. Constitution or human life. They are committed by people who have little respect for the consequences of misusing a gun to satisfy whatever they think is wrong in their lives. No wonder most gun owners get upset when "gun control" is mentioned.

Many of the recent shooters purchased their guns legally. They weren't terrorists or criminals by the standards we have now. Would a thorough risk assessment by an insurance company have made a difference? A risk assessment considering mental stability and destabilizing events in their life might have prevented the purchase of the guns that were used. If nothing else, it would have delayed the purchase, possibly enough to defuse the anger behind the shooting event. The insurance company, examining factors that a standard background check doesn't, might have prevented the sale entirely.

Gun owners get quite angry when asked to compromise even a little. "Why should WE be punished for the actions of a small handful of people? We're responsible gun owners!!" They have a point. However, they refuse to look at the fact that eventually the threshold will be crossed. People will DEMAND that something be done, and when that threshold is reached, SOMETHING will be done. I'm confident that the SOMETHING will be extreme measures in the eyes of gun owners. It will be sweeping. Rather a small compromise now that actually solves the problem, than a larger one later.

This idea is a very small compromise since it doesn't restrict purchasing or owning a gun. It does not infringe on the 2nd Amendment in any way. It only requires people to back up the claim of being a responsible gun owner. It requires a change of thinking, not a change in possession.

Ammo & Accessories

Where this idea will have the most immediate results is in the purchasing of bullets. Even an illegal gun needs ammo or it's a paperweight. You want ammo? Go buy ammo. Go buy all the ammo you want. BUT, you'll need your registration and insurance card. All ammo purchases will be attached to a legally registered and insured gun. If you own a medium range 9mm handgun, no one will have a problem with you buying a box or two of bullets for that gun. If you want to buy an extra clip, it gets added on to your insurance policy with little mention. If you want to buy 10 clips and enough bullets to fill those clips, you're going to need to explain it to your insurance agent.

If you own a 9mm and go in to buy bullets for an AR-15, you're going to get a phone call from your insurance agent. There'll be some questions about why you're trying to buy bullets for a gun you have not registered or insured. It will be a serious red flag and might even result in a call from law enforcement. They're going to be very curious about whose AR-15 you're buying bullets for, or the AR-15 that for some reason, you, a law-abiding, responsible individual, have failed to legally register and insure.

If a criminal is in possession of a handgun, he's going to need bullets or his gun is worthless. That means someone who has that same type of gun will need to go out on a limb to buy bullets for him. Eventually, that person is going to get that phone call from their insurance agent or law enforcement. Reducing guns to law-abiding citizens who register and insure their guns will make a huge difference. Making it difficult to acquire bullets, will make even black market guns and DIY guns a challenge for criminals. This one part of my idea may make the biggest difference of all in reducing gun violence. It won't eliminate it entirely. But, yeah, kinda. I believe this might make the most difference of all.

Some accessories will actually reduce your insurance. A carrying case or storage case for example. Some accessories will make the insurance go up. A high capacity magazine for example. If you want an accessory like that, fine, go buy one. The 2nd amendment says you have the right. But when we start changing the conversation to liability and responsibility, we're going to notice a fact that I have not heard discussed. The overwhelming majority of gun owners, who are highly responsible with their guns, are less often the ones buying accessories like that. And even if they do, so what? This group - the overwhelming majority of gun owners, who have shown a strong history of being responsible gun owners - are still unlikely to harm others with their guns. The other group - the ones we NEED to target because they have a history of irresponsibility, or have not shown that they can be completely trusted with such a weapon - will still find difficulty meeting the standards necessary to purchase the accessories, even if they somehow managed to meet those standards to get the insurance for the weapon. It's likely that the desire to purchase a high capacity magazine will be just enough to push him over the threshold of calculated risks and his insurance for the weapon itself could be revoked.

Bottom line, attaching ammo and accessories to a specific gun and gun owner further achieves the goals of this idea. The low risks of the overwhelming majority of safe gun owners doesn't change. The risks of the small minority of gun owners that are potentially dangerous, is further brought to the surface and helps to "self-weed" them from the population of gun owners.

Black Market

Of course, a black market will be energized by this idea. But, the very parts of this plan that energizes a black market, also give us the tools to defeat that black market by making it unnecessary and undesirable.

How do you defeat a black market? With allies. How do you gain allies? Money and teamwork. The teamwork comes from getting everyone on board with the same language of responsibility, instead of rights. When we change the language, we change the behavior. Change the language and we create motivation to comply. When we stop talking about the right to have a gun and focus on the responsibility of gun ownership, we create a team that is all on the same page. From the marketing of gun manufacturers, down to signage in retail locations, responsibility is the message and compliance is how we are responsible. When gun shows are full of lawyers and insurance companies, we will flood the culture with allies.

Alcohol producers all have a "drink responsibly" message in their advertising. This subtle and simple message is often credited with playing a role in the dramatic reduction in drunk driving since it's inception. A comparable message regarding gun ownership could have the same impact. Changing the mindset from rights to responsibility is our greatest asset in the long-term success of this idea.

Our second tool to defeat a black market is money. When gun sellers can make money from helping people comply with the idea, they will become our biggest allies. We NEED gun sellers on our side because they are our first contact with current gun owners. There are opportunities right out of the gate to pad the invoice and increase their bottom line. They can charge for registrations. They can charge for transferring registrations. They can facilitate sales between private individuals. They can offer classes, required with every sale. It would be a major conflict of interest to sell insurance, but I imagine they will find ways to partner with insurance companies. I imagine that as this idea becomes more comfortable, gun retailers will find multiple ways of increasing profits and benefits, all the while serving their customers. It will snowball.

All the while, those who would develop a black market will find their numbers shrinking. Their only customer base will be those who cannot get insurance legally. That includes criminals and risky individuals in a small set of people who want a gun. This idea has successfully targeted that group and prevented sales to most (if not all) of the people who would do others harm. If the insurance makes a gun cost prohibitive to purchase legally, imagine the cost of a gun on the black market. It will be a seller's market, even as sellers run out of customers.

Last, as part of the changing mindset, could we change the relationships between government and gun owners and gun sellers? As it is, government is viewed as kind of an adversary. Government is there to take guns away. Once people z that government is there to HELP responsible citizens achieve a legal path to gun ownership, could the relationship become one of partnership? Such a partnership could be a tremendous aide in the capture and prosecution of black market sellers. The easiest way to build such partnerships is for ATF agents to make regular visits to gun shops. Do it the same way as an outside sales rep might go around checking on customers. Take donuts. Go in with the attitude, "How can I help you be more successful / profitable?" Make friends. Friends achieve common goals.

School Shootings

School shootings are possibly the ones that disturb us the most. Teenagers, completely off the radar of law enforcement, taking a weapon to school for reasons that the adults around them overlooked or discounted. The adults who care most fail to recognize that a child they are close to is in danger.

On any given day, a high school student - ANY HIGH SCHOOL STUDENT - could be diagnosed with some kind of mental illness. Hormones half way between child and adult, mixed with social anxiety and the pressure to succeed with their grades or extracurriculars, is a recipe for an overwhelming level of stress. Then add bullies. And now, cyber-bullies, which are worst of all. It's a miracle more kids aren't taking a gun to school.

Instead of assuming, "My kid would NEVER do that," they will be faced with the possibility that, yes, their kid might do that. With few exceptions, even when there were red flags among friends and schoolmates, the parents never saw it coming.

The first way this will greatly impact school shootings is that registration and insurance introduces LIABILITY to the field.

Underage teenagers cannot sign a contract for the insurance. Just as with car insurance, the teenagers will be considered on the parents policy. For the parents to keep their insurance, the rates might go up. Or, the insurance company may require additional steps. All along, the conversation isn't about rights, it's about responsibility. When faced with the brutal reality that THEY are liable for what their teen does with their gun(s), several things will change.

Second, they will secure the guns differently to prevent the teen from having free access without the parent.

The third way this may reduce school shootings is in possible peripheral requirements. The insurance company, performing their due diligence for insuring their client, might also pay attention to certain red flags that are possibly overlooked now. They might communicate with the teen's school. Interview teachers, school counselors and other members of the faculty. Their relationship with the parents might involve greater communication. Each conversation will reinforce the responsibility of the parents, and further back up my first reason that insurance will make a difference. Currently, an outside risk assessor is missing. A thorough risk assessment might present a very different picture to the parents who believe "My kid would NEVER do that." But, the insurance company, in performing that due diligence, may actually catch the signs that lead to the violence before the violence takes place.

Could they require counseling for the teen to maintain the insurance coverage. Yes. Could the insurance company require access to notes from the therapist? Yes. Could they make it impossible for a parent to get insurance in the future? Possibly, yes. Faced with never being able to own a gun, possibly having to get rid of any guns they presently own can be a strong deterrent to non compliance. They might curse the insurance company. But, they will comply. They WILL take steps to reduce the likelihood that their teen will harm others.

Schools might require proof of insurance (and even proof of safety testing) before students can attend school. Parents who might try to dodge responsibility will be forced to comply with insurance requirements. Again, they will curse the insurance companies.   But,   they   WILL comply.

Or, we could just arm all the teachers. Let's look at how that might go.

A middle-aged teacher in Anytown, America has been teaching English to 9th graders for 30 years. She's an outstanding teacher and her students love her. One day, we hand her a gun and teach her how to shoot it. We tell her that "in the event of a live shooter, use your gun and take him out." Do we honestly expect that's how it will work out? Hundreds of panicked students with a handful of school faculty and administration, all armed. She's never shot or killed anyone, and now, she must "take out" a beloved student. Really?

In school shootings in the past, we have had a variety of heroes on the staff. Some died. Not because they did or didn't have a gun. But because they have a mindset to save the child, even when that child is trying to kill others. Some teachers might be able to pull the trigger. They can justify it and say they are protecting the other students, which is correct. But in that scenario, can we honestly expect every teacher to feel that way?

We can also have the possible scenario of a live shooter and half a dozen teachers grab their guns. They received a cursory level of training 4 years earlier and haven't been to the range since. Now, they're going to be heroes. One of them gets the live shooter all right. But in the process, they take out 5 other students and 2 of the would-be heroes actually shoot each other. Shooter: 7. Armed teachers 7.

The Insurance

Insurance companies are the best there is for assessing risk of individuals. Statistics that most people might never think of factor into the rates for car insurance, home owners, health and business insurance. The same would apply to gun ownership. Insurance companies would factor in a set of criteria and determine a rate for that individual, for that gun. Insurance rates will be based on risk like any other type of insurance.

Have you ever noticed that insurance companies NEVER lose money? They are freaky smart with assessment of risk and before they write that policy, they already know the devil they are contracting with, maybe even better than a person knows themselves. Most people don't recognize their own risky or sketchy behavior. The insurance company will spot it immediately and charge accordingly. There may be ways to get your rates down, either through lifestyle changes or other changes a person can make.

For responsible people, the cost of the insurance will be minimal. Many gun owners ALREADY have insurance as a rider on other policies they may have. If they are as responsible as they say, the perceived "punishment" will be so minor as to be a non factor. It is possible, they are already paying for it.

If you're as responsible as you say, back that up. DO something besides claim how responsible you are. Compliance does that. And, it says to the left "We ARE responsible." Responsible people rarely do irresponsible things. They won't let their kids play with the guns. They won't let a friend borrow their guns. They will protect their word that they are responsible because they know that the consequences are theirs.

Don't like the cost? Shop around. The insurance companies, as an industry, will set standards just like they do with any other kind of insurance. Prices, coverage and criteria for coverage may vary slightly company to company. But, as long as a minimal legal coverage threshold is met, it's no problem. Many insurance companies offer financing now. They might actually be able to finance the gun right along with the monthly insurance premium. THAT could result in more guns. However, more guns in the hands of responsible people does not translate into more of a gun problem.

People with sketchy pasts, of any kind, will not be able to get insurance. Period. Without insurance, they will not be able to buy a gun. Yes, there will still be some illegal gun sales and some illegal guns. No solution can be expected to eliminate the issue 100%. However, this plan will make it far more difficult for sketchy people to buy a gun. And, it has minimum inconvenience and restriction for responsible gun owners and sellers. At minimum, the cost of the insurance will make the gun cost prohibitive for the potential buyer with a sketchy past, while barely effecting those who have a history of being responsible citizens.

A parent with a gun (or guns), paying a premium for that gun that includes coverage for him having children in the house... Or, a person who can't get insurance because of a mental illness, or self-control concerns who has guns that shouldn't... Someone with a history of irresponsibility... Of course, there are many factors that indicate if a person is likely to be responsible or not. The insurance companies would be able to consider ALL of those factors.

We have SR-22 insurance for people who have lost their driver's license. Why couldn't the same be applied to guns? Such policies also mean that rebuilding a responsible history is possible. Drivers who drive safe for a period of time can drop the SR-22 insurance. The same would apply to gun ownership for people who have made mistakes. Think about all the people who now own a gun, who have no plans to become more responsible in their lives. Could the desire to own a gun motivate more responsible behavior from those citizens in other ways? Possibly.

Parents will think twice before they leave the semi-automatic where the teenagers can get it. Many people who want a gun to "compensate" for something, will think twice. Impulse buying will see a sharp decline when the gun show is full of lawyers and accountants selling insurance and talking about liability. In the end, the system will self-weed many of those who shouldn't have a gun. Not all, because there will always be people with more resources than brains and skills. But many.

You know what breaks many teenage boys from driving reckless? The day that the parents make him start paying for his own car insurance. On that day, the kid becomes a man and has to pay for his mistakes, and, reaps the rewards for good behavior. If he doesn't have an accident, his rates go down. When he understands that, his driving gets better. Cue the singing angels. When he starts having to put gas in the car and consider the points on his license, he suddenly realizes that an accident might actually happen to him if he doesn't drive like a grown up. Not all young people learn the lesson, but many do.

Facing and accepting responsibility changes behavior. No additional legislation or rules are necessary.

In The Event Of A Shooting...

In the event of a shooting, the process for law enforcement won't change. They will still investigate the shooting as a potential crime until they can eliminate any criminal intent or violation of the law.

If the shooting is determined to be criminal, the shooter is guaranteed a quality defense attorney and a fair trial with a jury of his (or her) peers. These things won't change.

The insurance coverage might include funds for a private, criminal defense attorney, and might even assist with related costs of preparing a defense. Coverage might include compensation to the family while the shooter is incarcerated or on trial. Expenses that would otherwise be entirely the burden of the shooter's family.

Coverage might also include a separate investigation into the shooting, which could be used to assist the defense team. Or possibly, a separate investigation might exonerate the shooter. An investigation might also decide the limits of the coverage and how far they are willing to go with their support. Insurance is a contract. Their investigation might decide if the contract has been broken.

Insurance coverage might also include a defense team if there is a civil trial, where a defendant is not guaranteed an attorney by the state. Insuring a gun owner implies their support of that gun owner and confidence that they aren't going to a anyone without cause. If they believe in their client, providing for a defense team in the civil trial would be a natural benefit of their coverage. In the event of losing such a civil trial, the insurance company pays that settlement just as it works with auto and other types of liability insurance coverage.

The NRA

An interesting aspect of this idea will be that the NRA will have a worthy opponent to battle with them. You know what beats a gun in a knife fight? Lawyers. The insurance industry will go head-to-head with the NRA over our gun ownership. Can you imagine the two battling it out for votes from politicians? Get your popcorn!!

I don't actually have any problems whatsoever with the NRA. They have done very, very, very well what they are supposed to do. ALL groups should be so effective. The problem is that we don't have an equally effective group with a different agenda balancing out the gun issue. Like most problems, the answer lies somewhere in the middle and will only be achieved when both extremes compromise a little. Right now, the other side consists of individuals and groups with a lot less power. Could the insurance industry be that balancing force? I think they could, even though they wouldn't actually be an opposing one.

I can't think of any other issue in this country where a single advocate has accomplished as much as the NRA. My problem is that they create and receive such firm adherence to their mission that all conversation on the issue stalls. They polarize their membership so passionately to the right, that it makes it difficult to even have a conversation on change.

It's become this way because there is no strong second advocate with a different message. Sure, there is a very large left side. As Americans, we seem to be split very evenly. But those Americans, as small, individual voices, have nowhere the weight of one powerful, well-funded advocate on the right. The insurance industry could provide that voice - even though they are not actually an opposing voice in any way. Even if my idea isn't the answer, having a strong different advocate will balance the conversation and we can hopefully come up with an idea that IS even better.

The message from this strong second advocate will single-handedly change the narrative. Insurance companies don't care about removing all the guns - certainly not if each gun is a customer. They also have no interest in everyone becoming armed because their risks increase exponentially. They talk about responsibility. They talk about liability. This is the change of perspective that the issue needs to remove the polarization we have now.

We have thousands of traffic accidents every day. With laws that we all agree to and a system that seems to work effectively, there's no national news coverage for these accidents. There are no rallies. There are no advocacy groups to end driving - or, to give everyone a car. There is little drama over the issue. When we have an agreeable system to improve responsibility and the legislation is correctly directed where it needs to be, this issue will also stop being in the national news fueling both sides to further polarize. Unpolarized, we might come up with even better solutions than the one I am proposing.

The Government

One reason the 2nd Amendment advocates will lose their protest is because this plan gets the government out of the equation. The whole concept behind the 2nd Amendment was not so people could protect their homes. It was to protect against a failed government. It was to protect the people from a return to feudal systems in Europe. If the government failed - and in the 1770s, democracy was truly an experiment - the people had the means to start over. Any action that suggests that the government is going to start taking guns will be a rallying cry for every gun owner.

The right objects to any sort of legislation that could, in effect, take their guns away or restrict their right to purchase and own a gun. This plan would not do that. If someone wants a gun, go buy a gun. Buy any gun you want. Buy as many guns as you want. Just, make sure you have insurance on it, register it properly and confirm that you know how to operate it properly. It's hard to argue that the government is trying to take your gun if the government tells people to go buy a gun if they want one.

Which leads to the argument, "They start with a small restriction and then they add to it whenever the government wants to." That could be true. The counter would be that if we reduce gun violence and deaths, there'll be no need to take further action. If there are fewer deaths and shootings, even the far left side will not feel a need to do anything additional. However, if nothing is done, the worst fears of the gun owners will eventually come to be.

It's possible that peripheral laws could be instituted. However, they would all return to the basic simple law regarding insurance, registration and training. Peripheral laws might create penalties for non-compliance, or clearly define what the consequences are for improper use of a gun. We have laws for some criminal offenses that are reasonably clear and prosecutable. Those laws vary state-to-state though.

Laws regarding guns should be nationwide and universal. When gun advocates use an amendment to the U.S. constitution as the basis for their argument, any laws regarding guns should also be U.S. wide. To avoid people skirting the law in one state by buying their gun in another state, this basic law needs to be universal from state to state.

As for the government, HIPPA protects medical information. Gun sellers and law enforcement have no access to a person's medical information to verify if they should be restricted from having a gun. We WANT to restrict gun access of those who have some types of mental illness, but currently cannot effectively do that. Without criminal cause, we cannot weigh their medical records. Simply having a mental illness doesn't give a criminal cause. Therefore, all the legislation in the world that focuses on background checks, fails to address one of the most important factors.

Same is true for extremists. There are watch lists. But, unless they have been convicted of a crime, the government has little legal ability to restrict that person from purchasing a gun. Criminal history is about the only thing the government currently has available. If they do not have a conviction, no red flag. I personally believe that the RIGHT to have a gun should only extend to U.S. citizens.

Insurance companies are NOT the government. They can ask anything they want to perform a risk assessment. And because they are not the government, and generally a local agent that people get to know, people might be a little more forthcoming with the information they provide. Maybe, maybe not. But without the information, they don't get the insurance. Insurance companies can access a variety of records now to determine that risk and verify the information they need. If a person is dishonest or not forthcoming, their insurance is denied or revoked. Revoked insurance means the guns are not legally possessed and the government can step in to enforce the law. Get insurance and get your guns back. Wait too long, the guns are auctioned or destroyed.

The insurance must be purchased PRIOR to the purchase of the gun. That means someone contacted their agent during normal business hours, agreed on the price of the coverage and paid it, AFTER the agent was able to perform the necessary risk assessment and determine that price. Proof of the insurance is provided to the insured. And then, the gun purchaser is able to go purchase their gun. At the gun store, the seller is able to verify that insurance with a quick phone call, or a database online.

Along with the proof of insurance, restrictions may be included. The safety test for example. The seller may offer that safety test on the spot, or can schedule the buyer for the test later within a designated period of time. Failure to take the test means the insurance gets immediately revoked and the gun must immediately. The seller would provide the registration on the spot. They will also state on the database whether the safety test was completed.

Gun Sales

We have legislation now. Endless volumes of legislation. Gun sellers complain about the difficulty of compliance. Checking on prospective gun purchasers is often challenging. The system works, sort of. If it's up to date, or the system isn't down or something else leaving them unable to do as required at the point of sale. Insurance companies already have the internal structure in place for claims and customer service to provide confirmation of insurance coverage 24/7.

The current system is also lacking when it comes to private sales of guns and sales of guns at gun shows. Requiring insurance is a simple system that ANY person selling a gun can comply with. No one needs to be a registered gun seller, or any kind of restrictions like that. ANYONE can buy or sell a gun. Just verify the insurance to protect yourself and keep it legal. This system will prevent many impulse sales.

The seller may (and probably will) charge a small fee for verifying insurance, or performing the necessary registration. They could include it in the cost of the gun. When you buy a new car, there are a number of fees that few people ever question. Same would apply to purchasing a gun.

The government will provide filing of all sales and transfers of guns through private sales. There could be a small form (3-4 questions) that could be filled out online. It would verify the information from person A to person B. It would verify the insurance information. And, it would verify the gun information.

In all private sales, the purchaser will be required (in a set, reasonable time) to visit a verified gun shop and formally register that gun properly and in their name. There should be a form that people can download to document any gun sales. Or, an online form that people can fill out to document the sale and keep the chain of ownership properly registered. There are probably several ways to efficiently handle this process. However, the SELLER maintains liability until the BUYER completes the registration process and their insurance can be verified.

It's also possible that legal gun sellers could offer "transfers" as a service. Person A wants to sell their gun to Person B. Go to a gun store and they can handle the sale legally, on the spot, including transfer of the registration and the safety training. If a seller has any nervousness about the person they are selling the gun to, this might be the safest way to do it.

Gun sellers, if they are smart and enterprising business owners, will find all kinds of ways to capitalize on this system. Everything they do to make money off this system will further cement the system and make it work even better. Everything they do will further change the conversation from rights, to responsibility.

Manufacturers

Something I can imagine from this is the work of manufacturers. Car makers have made cars safer and more difficult to steal. Every year, we, the consumers, get cars that reduce the likelihood of accidents and injuries. Would gun manufacturers also take steps to make guns safer? Could the insurance requirement cause such a change?

The changes in autos were brought about by the demands of consumers as well as insurance companies. Gun manufacturers would be faced with similar demands. Gun purchasers would want their insurance rates to go down and so would demand guns that are safer. Insurance companies, to give their customers what they want, would also demand safer guns.

I believe it's possible that an evolution in guns could take place that actually makes guns safer. Right now, with no second advocate, there is little motivation for that evolution to occur.

A safety feature I'd love to see is a Super RFID chip. Lost or stolen guns could be located in minutes, before they are used illegally by criminals. Imagine a police officer performing a routine traffic stop. The officer could scan the vehicle and would know if there are any guns in the vehicle. An RFID reader at the perimeter of a school's property could alert those inside and safety measures could begin before a shooter even made it to the building. A gun could be programmed to the registered owner and no one else would be able to fire that gun. If such a safety feature could be installed later, it brings the risk factors down significantly, and thus, greatly reduces the cost of the insurance. Everyone wins.

Another reason that cars got safer is competition. One car maker introduces a safety feature and car buyers flock to their showrooms, causing all other car makers to play catch up. Marketing of guns will change along with the rest of the language. Instead of language about what the gun can do, the language might become about the features that will reduce the cost of insurance. Guns and safety in the same conversation? Yes. When we change the focus to responsibility.

A gun is purchased for the safety of the gun owner. When we change the conversation from entitlement, all sides can work together to achieve that.

When a gun is manufactured, the registration and insurance process begins. The manufacturer must register EVERY gun produced and have insurance on it. When they sell those guns to a distributor, the distributor must transfer the registration and insurance. Then, to a dealer. Then to a retailer. At each step, the insurance and registration must carry with each, individual gun. This will reduce the number of black market guns and guns without a registered owner. Every gun must have SOMEONE responsible for it, at every step from the manufacturer to the end consumer. Every gun. Every step.

Illegal Guns and Gun Sales

Here in the Chicago area, we have many people crossing state lines to buy a gun. Illinois has some of the most restrictive gun laws in the nation, but an hour drive avoids those laws. A FEDERAL law, simple as it is, makes it unnecessary and a waste of time to go to Indiana to buy a gun. The purchaser will still need to register the gun in the state they live in, which might be tricky in Indiana. They will still need to complete a training course, which turns that 1 hour drive into an afternoon, or longer, if the course cannot be completed that day. And, an insurance agent cannot sell insurance on a gun purchased in another state. An insurance agent in Indiana is unlikely to sell insurance to someone who does not live in Indiana. it might even send a red flag to the insurance company that could cause the agent to review other policies they have written for that customer. Guns being purchased in one state and taken home to another state will mostly end.

A black market may focus on providing guns with no questions asked. But as gun manufacturers become compliant, and distributors, and wholesalers and resellers become compliant, the number of guns available for a black market will shrink dramatically. The only sources will be independent manufacturers and international manufacturers willing to skirt the rules and ship to customers here. But in a short time, law enforcement will be able to restrict those manufacturers and limit their ability to deliver a product to a customer here. Some will still get through. But in time, the impact would shrink dramatically.

That leaves 3D printed guns and other DIY guns. There are designs available online that allows a person to print a complete gun. These guns do not have serial numbers and are of materials that can slip through a metal detector. How would this plan effect those? We would have to pressure the people who publish those designs to do more. We can shut down the websites and they will pop back up somewhere else. This will be the greatest challenge for law enforcement. It is already a growing challenge with the legislation we have now. Maybe increasing the consequences for unregistered guns of this type will make a difference. If unregistered guns and uninsured guns are a crime, it makes these guns a crime to manufacture and possess. Are these guns illegal now?

Gun Time-Out & Pawn Shops

In some cases, the cost of insurance may exceed the amount a gun owner can pay. Maybe they lose their job, or have medical bills, or some other bills that have higher priority. In a case like that, they can turn some, or all, of their guns into an approved armory for safe storage.

It might also be an option is someone has teenagers at home. To reduce their risks, they may choose to store some of the guns until the teens are out of school. Taking a summer vacation? Store the guns while you're gone.

The storage facility must meet certain security standards to protect against theft and armed robbery, by both inside and out agents. This armory can also handle transfers of inventory from wholesalers to retailers. It might also handle evidence storage for law enforcement, as a private contractor.

Storage will be coordinated by the insurance company when the premium isn't paid. And, retrieving guns from storage, once all premiums are caught up, will also be handled by the insurance company. The gun owner is not involved in any way, to prevent temptation. It also gives the gun owner some deniability should a theft be attempted at the armory. Guns may also be turned in at pre-approved locations, such as resellers that can coordinate with the insurance company for pick up and drop off.

Cost of storage can be determined by the insurance company, but should not be a prohibitive amount. As always, the purpose is never to take away someone's gun(s). The purpose of insurance is never to be a vehicle to take away anyone's guns. This step provides a measure in between non-compliance and absolute surrender of their guns. This entire plan is to respect those who hold on to the 2nd Amendment as gospel, and absolutely, 100%, do not want to surrender their gun(s)

Although a time limit of so many months (for example) should be imposed, that is between the gun owner and the insurance company.

Pawn shops are going to have a problem with this system. Taking in a gun temporarily, or without taking over ownership, will not be possible. Every gun must be registered to the owner and be insured. If you transfer the registration to the pawn shop, isn't that the same as selling it? A pawn shop might be willing to transfer the registration and insure that gun, but how does that effect the amount they "loan" the gun owner? How can we still call it a loan if the pawn shop holds the registration and insurance?

No. A pawn shop system will not work. It leaves too much wiggle-room in keeping accurate registration and ownership records. Too much turnover with insurance. Too much deniability of liability. Too many lost guns or paperwork that never made it through the system. No. Pawn shops are out.

However, legal gun sellers may be able to work out a temporary buy-back program of some kind since they are already insured and already familiar with the registration process. To legally keep the registration and insurance properly attached to possession of the gun, it would have to be a buy-back system and not a loan system. The gun shop might be willing to hold the gun for a monthly fee. Guns held like this would be transferred to the armory until the gun owner decides to sell or they miss a payment. Terms for missing a payment and forfeiting a gun could be determined independently by each gun seller.

Prosecution

With only the one law, we give the rules clarity. Prosecution may have a variety of levels and elements (1st or 2nd Degree, felony, misdemeanor, aggravated, etc.). But, the law itself will be simple. The simpler it is, the simpler it is to follow AND to prosecute when it isn't followed.

To facilitate compliance by law abiding citizens, a website could be established for people to register guns online (might be tricky to figure out the gun rifling thing) and to handle sales online. It could be as simple as an app on a smart phone. The simpler and more convenient, the more compliance and the less resistance by gun advocates, gun sellers and gun owners. Even with sales like this, the SELLER retains liability until the sale is completed. Completion means the BUYER has legally registered and insured the gun in their name.

And, the old claim that only criminals will have guns will lose its merit. It won't happen immediately. But gradually, criminals will have more and more difficulty getting a gun. The back market will attempt to fill this void. However, if gun manufacturers are compliant, a black market will be limited. Independent manufacturers and 3D printed guns will become more common to fill the void. The balance for that will be that a dramatic reduction in other types of gun crime and other crimes involving guns, will leave a void in law enforcement. Could the time and effort for one be transferred to prosecution of those like the independents and 3D designers?

Responsible gun owners will be careful about what happens to their gun and where it ends up, reducing the criminal element in possession. With each arrest, a gun (or guns) will be confiscated and destroyed and we will be left MOSTLY with guns in the hands of responsible people, not criminals. Right now, there are THOUSANDS of unregistered guns on the street. Gradually, most of those will be found and destroyed. Not overnight, of course, but in time.

Simplicity will be highly motivating for compliance. It will be easier to comply with the law than to not comply. Penalties must be strict and severe to provide sufficient deterrent. Without such prosecution, we make no progress. Without meaningful consequences, the law has no weight.

Follow The Money

When this begins to turn the tide, what will happen to the money spent on advocacy? Billions of dollars might suddenly stop. Smart advertising redirects that cash to further the message. Television ads that talk about responsibility and thank all those who have done the right thing with their guns (registration and insurance) will keep the snowball rolling in the right direction. Sure. Call it market manipulation. But, we could do a lot worse with the money.

In the best of all outcomes, though, that money will get redirected to help with the cost of counseling for all those teenagers now required to have counseling. The irony is that most of this money was going to left-sided advocacy groups and the people who will need support for counseling are people who own guns and have teenagers. Funny how the circle works, but directing that money to help this way will only further engrain the insurance plan. The cost of that counseling could be prohibitive. Not only will you have a responsible gun owner losing their gun(s), you have a teenager that needs therapy not getting it - unless these funds are redirected.

Conclusion

Confidence that responsible people are acting responsibly. That's what we want, right? This plan addresses the root cause - the mindset. It isn't about control or restriction. As Americans, we want freedom and choices. What makes The United States the greatest country ever is our freedom. No one wants to infringe upon that - even the left. We just want to keep people that would harm others away from the guns with minimal inconvenience to responsible people. We want fewer people to die from gun violence. This plan would do that.

Along with this plan, we can expect a change in the mindset of needing a gun and using a gun. The current thinking is extremely binary. Either, we all need a gun and should force people to be polite to us by letting them know we're armed. Or, just do away with all the guns. By changing this polarizing mindset, more people might decide they don't need a gun and that people are plenty polite when we're not threatening them. In addition to accomplishing the goal of reducing the number of deaths from gun violence, we might actually accomplish the bigger goal of seeing that we can resolve problems when we stop locking ourselves down on opposite sides.